The Great Exhale

OrangeBooks Publication

1st Floor, Rajhans Arcade, Mall Road, Kohka, Bhilai, Chhattisgarh 490020
Website: **www.orangebooks.in**

First Edition, 2026

ISBN: 978-93-7426-661-8

Price: Rs. 549.00

Printed in India

THE GREAT EXHALE

Notes on Finding your Place in a Loud World

KARLYN PRAKASH

OrangeBooks Publication
www.orangebooks.in

To every woman.

Who has ever held her breath to keep the peace,

this is your exhale.

To my Husband.

Thank you for loving the woman I was and welcoming the woman I have become.

Disclaimer

The information contained in this book is for educational, entertainment, and inspirational purposes only. It is not intended as a substitute for professional medical advice, diagnosis, or treatment, or for professional psychological or psychiatric counseling. The author and publisher encourage you to seek professional help when needed and disclaim any liability for any loss or damage resulting from the use of the information contained in this book.

Cover Design by: Karlyn Prakash

Author's Note

This book began as a series of whispers to myself.

For a long time, I lived my life in a state of high-functioning exhaustion. I was checking all the boxes. I was climbing the ladder. I was managing the family, the career, and the expectations of everyone around me; on paper, I was a success.

In reality, I was holding my breath.

I started my blog, *Letters from the Sixth Sky*, not because I had found the answers, but because I was desperate for a new perspective.

I felt like I was living on the ground floor of a very noisy building—stuck in the traffic of petty arguments, paralyzed by the fear of "what if," and weighed down by the need to be "good." I needed to find a way to rise above the fog. I needed to find an altitude where I could breathe.

The "Sixth Sky" became my metaphor for that place of clarity. It is the place where the noise fades and the truth become visible.

I wrote this book in the margins of a real, messy life. I wrote it on days when I felt wise, and I wrote it on days when I felt like I was falling apart. I am not writing to you from a mountaintop of perfection. I am writing to you from the kitchen table, likely with a pile of laundry behind me that I have decided to ignore for the sake of my sanity.

I am not a guru. I am a fellow traveler who simply decided to stop carrying the heavy bags.

If you are reading this, chances are you are the "Strong One." You are the one people call when things break. You are the one who holds it all together.

My hope is that within these pages, you find a place where you are allowed to put it down. My hope is that you realize that you do not have to earn your rest, and you do not have to apologize for your evolution.

We are all just walking to each other's home. Let's walk a little lighter.

Karlyn Prakash

(*Creator of Letters from the Sixth Sky)*

Introduction
The Art of Arrival

I know you are tired.

It is not just physical tiredness that comes from a long week or a sleepless night. It is a deeper, ancient kind of exhaustion. It is the exhaustion of a woman who has spent decades holding her breath.

For the first half of our lives, we are taught that life is a performance. We are handed a script before we can even read, and we memorize our lines perfectly.

- **The Nice Girl:** The one who smiles when she is angry, who apologizes for taking up space, and who measures her worth by how accommodating she can be.
- **The Fixer:** The one who carries everyone else's emotional backpacks, believing that if she just works hard enough, she can save people from their own choices.
- **The General Manager of the Universe:** The one who lies awake at 3 AM, trying to mentally control the weather, the stock market, and her children's future.

We climb the Ladder of success. We chase visible trophies. We treat our bodies like renovation projects and our time like an infinite resource. We do everything right.

Then, somewhere around the halfway point, we get to the top of the ladder, look around, and realize, “I am cold up here, and I am lonely.”

We realize that we have built a life that looks perfect on paper but feels heavy in our bones.

This book is about what happens next.

It is about the moment you decide to put the heavy suitcase down. It is about the moment you decide to stop climbing the Ladder and start building a Campfire, trading the desire to be "impressive" for the desire to be warm.

This is not a book about adding more to your to-do list. You have enough lists. This is a book about The Great Unlearning.

It is about unlearning the lie that you are responsible for everyone’s happiness. It is about unlearning the fear of the "Hallway"; that scary, messy space between who you were and who you are becoming. It is about making friends with your own mortality, not to scare you, but to wake you up to the vibrant, urgent beauty of the time you have left.

We are going to talk about the "Sixth Sky," a place of perspective where you can watch the storms of life without drowning in them. We are going to talk about leaving a legacy not of stone monuments, but of invisible ripples of kindness.

This process, this shedding, this realigning, this softening is not a crisis. It is an arrival.

You are not falling behind. You are not losing your edge. You are simply returning to the original version of yourself, the one who existed before the world told you who to be.

You don't need to hold it all together anymore. You don't need to be the "Nice Girl" anymore. You have permission to rest.

Take a deep breath.

Welcome to The Exhale.

✦

Contents

Part I
The Shedding
(The Art of Un-Becoming)

There is a sculpture by Michelangelo called the Atlas Slave. It is an unfinished piece, depicting a man struggling to emerge from a heavy block of stone. He is not being built; he is being revealed. The stone is being chipped away to show the man who was already there.

For the first half of our lives, we are not the statue; we are the stone collectors.

We spend decades adding layers to ourselves. We layer on the "Nice Girl" who never makes a fuss. We layer on the "Fixer" who carries everyone else's problems. We layer on the "General Manager" who tries to control the uncontrollable. We drape ourselves in expectations, believing that the heavier we are, the more valuable we become.

But there comes a tipping point. It often arrives quietly. You wake up one morning, look at the life you have painstakingly built, and you feel a profound exhaustion that sleep cannot fix. You realize that the heaviness you feel is not the weight of the world; it is the weight of the layers you are wearing.

This section is not about self-improvement. It is about self-retrieval.

It is about looking at the heavy suitcase of resentment you have dragged around for years and finally setting it down. It is about realizing that "No" is a complete sentence. It is about dropping the rope in the tug-of-war you can never win.

We are going to chip away the stone. We are going to hold a funeral for the version of you that tried to please everyone, and we are going to introduce you to the woman underneath.

It is time to let go.

Chapter 1
The Joy of Being Misunderstood

For most of my life, I operated like a one-person Public Relations firm.

If someone looked at me the wrong way, I wanted to fix it. If someone misinterpreted my silence as anger, I rushed to explain that I was just tired. If someone thought I was making a mistake, I prepared a mental PowerPoint presentation of reasons to prove I was being strategic.

I spent decades trying to control the narrative. I thought that if I could just explain myself clearly enough, everyone would understand me. If they understood me, they would like me. If they liked me, I would be safe.

It is exhausting work, managing your own reputation in the minds of everyone you meet. It is a full-time job with terrible pay and no time off.

Then, the shift happened. It wasn't a sudden lightning bolt; it was more like a slow sunrise.

I realized that being understood is a luxury, not a necessity.

We grow up thinking that "understanding" is the bridge between people. We are taught that we must communicate until we are on the same page. But the truth is, some people are reading a completely different book …. and that is okay.

The High Cost of Over-Explaining

Think about the last time you felt the desperate need to explain yourself.

Maybe you were a teacher justifying your lesson plan to a skeptical parent. Maybe you were a business owner justifying your prices to a client who wanted a discount. Maybe you were simply telling a friend why you couldn't come to dinner.

Did you offer a simple "No"? Or did you offer a paragraph of excuses, apologies, and logical breakdowns?

When we over-explain, we are essentially saying: *"Please validate my existence. Please tell me I am allowed to make this choice."*

Every time you offer an unsolicited explanation, you leak energy. You are handing over your power. You are asking for permission to be yourself.

The realization I want to offer you is this: Your choices do not require courtroom defense. You do not need to call witnesses to prove that you are tired, or ambitious, or happy, or done. The fact that you feel it is evidence enough.

The Mirror Effect

Here is the hard truth that brings the most peace: People do not see you as you are; they see you as *they* are.

When someone calls you "too loud," they often reveal their own need for quiet. When someone calls you "too ambitious," they reveal their own comfort with stasis. When someone misinterprets your boundaries as selfishness, they are showing you their own lack of boundaries.

This applies to everyone. The academic who critiques your work harshly often critiquing their own insecurities. The relative who asks why you aren't married/rich/settled yet is often projecting their own roadmap onto your terrain.

You can spend your entire life trying to clean the mirror of their perception, trying to make them see the "real" you but you cannot clean a mirror that isn't yours.

Privacy vs. Secrecy

There is a fear that often comes up here. We worry that if we stop explaining, we become secretive or cold.

But there is a vast difference between secrecy and privacy.

- Secrecy is withholding the truth because you are ashamed.
- Privacy is withholding the truth because it is precious.

When you stop explaining your dreams to people who crush them, you aren't being secretive; you are protecting your seeds until they are strong enough to grow. When you stop explaining your pain to people who cannot offer empathy, you are not being cold; you are being wise. You are curating your audience.

The Freedom of "Letting Them Be Wrong"

There is a specific kind of power that comes when you stop correcting the record.

Imagine someone has a completely wrong idea about you. Maybe they think you are stuck-up because you are shy. Maybe they think you are lucky because they didn't see you working until 2 AM.

The old version of you would want to fight that. You would want to lay out the evidence.

The new version of you, the version that is exhaling simply shrugs.

You learn to say to yourself: *"They are allowed to be wrong about me."*

Letting people be wrong about you is the ultimate form of self-trust. It means your internal compass is so steady that you don't need a committee to tell you where North is. It means you know your own heart so well that you don't need to hand out maps to visitors.

Closing the PR Firm

When you resign from the job of managing other people's opinions, you get so much time back.

You get the time you used to spend replaying conversations in the shower. You get the energy you used to waste drafting mental text messages that you never sent. You get the space to simply *be*, rather than *perform*.

This doesn't mean you don't care about anyone. It doesn't mean you become unfeeling. In fact, it’s the opposite. When you stop trying to force people to understand you, you can finally just love them for who they are, without the transaction of validation.

So, let them misunderstand. Let them think about what they want. You have better things to do than manage the archives of their opinions. You have a life to live.

Chapter 2
The Death of the "Nice Girl"

There is a woman who lives inside many of us. I call her the "Nice Girl."

You know her. She is the one who apologizes when someone else bumps into her at the grocery store. She is the one who laughs at a joke she finds offensive just to keep the mood light. She is the one who says, *"Oh, it's no trouble at all!"* when asked to do a favor that is a massive amount of trouble.

The Nice Girl is a master of accommodation. She is a shape shifter. She walks into a room, reads the temperature, and adjusts her personality to make everyone else comfortable.

She is beloved. She is praised. She is "easy."

But at 40, I realized something terrifying: The Nice Girl was killing me.

She was killing my truth. She was killing my boundaries. She was killing my ability to be known because when you are busy being what everyone else wants, there is no room left to be who you are.

The Training Ground

We didn't come out of the womb this way. We were trained.

From the time we are small, especially as women, we are rewarded for being pleasant. We are told, *"Don't be bossy,"* while boys are told they are *"leaders."* We are told, *"Smile, it looks prettier,"* while boys are told to be tough.

We learned a very specific equation: Likeability = Safety.

We internalized the idea that if we are "difficult", if we have needs, if we have loud opinions, if we take up space, we will be rejected. So, we learned to shrink. We learned to smooth things over. We learned to swallow our anger until it turned into a hard knot in our stomachs.

Nice vs. Kind (The Crucial Difference)

The hardest part of killing the Nice Girl is the fear that we will become "mean."

However, there is a massive difference between being Nice and being Kind.

- Nice is a performance. It is rooted in fear. It is about pleasing others so they will like you. It is dishonest. When you say "Yes" to a dinner you hate, you are being nice, but you are lying.
- Kind is a practice. It is rooted in love and integrity. It is about truth.

Sometimes, the kindest thing you can do is tell the truth, even if it's uncomfortable.

- Nice keeps a friend in a bad relationship because you don't want to upset her. Kind tells her she deserves better.
- Nice agrees to a deadline you can't meet, causing chaos later. Kind says, *"I can't do that by Friday,"* allowing the team to plan effectively.

Niceness is flimsy; it breaks under pressure. Kindness is strong; it can hold the weight of the truth.

The "Fawn" Response

Psychologists talk about the "Fight or Flight" response to stress but there is a third response that women often default to: **Fawn.**

To "fawn" means to immediately try to please the threat to make it go away.

When a colleague speaks to you disrespectfully, the Nice Girl doesn't fight back. She giggles. She minimizes it. She "fawns." She tries to make the aggressor feel good so that she can be safe.

This is not a personality flaw. It is a survival instinct.

But you are not a child anymore. You are a grown woman. You do not need to fawn to survive. You have the power to stand your ground, keep your face neutral, and say, *"Please don't speak to me that way."*

The Corset

Living as the Nice Girl is like wearing a corset. It looks good from the outside, it holds everything in, it gives you a pleasing shape, but it restricts your breathing. It presses on your organs. It makes it impossible to take a full, deep breath.

The "Shedding" phase of life is about unlacing the corset.

When you first take it off, you might feel exposed. You might feel "sloppy" or "too much." You might worry that without the corset, people won't love you.

Then, you take that first deep breath. You feel your lungs expand to their full capacity. You realize that the people who only loved you when you were cinched tight and breathless were never really loving *you*, they loved the costume.

The Funeral

It is time to hold a funeral for the Nice Girl.

We don't need to be angry at her. We can thank her. She protected you when you were young. She helped you navigate middle school bullies and difficult bosses. She did her job.

However, she is too small for the woman you are now. She cannot hold the magnitude of your life.

So, we lay her to rest, and in her place, a new woman rises. A woman who is Kind, but not a doormat. A woman who is Generous, but not at the expense of her own depletion. A woman who is Real.

The Aftermath (Warning: People Will Be Annoyed)

I need to warn you: When you stop being the Nice Girl, people will be annoyed.

The people who benefit from your lack of boundaries will be upset when you start setting them. They will say, *"You've changed."* They will say, *"You're being difficult."*

Let them be annoyed.

Their annoyance is not evidence that you are doing something wrong. It is evidence that you are finally doing something right. You are breaking the contract that said you exist solely for their comfort.

You are reclaiming your voice, and a voice is a terrible thing to waste on just saying "I'm sorry."

Chapter 3
Resigning from the Job of "Fixer"

I used to believe that my love was measured by how much I could carry for other people.

If a friend was sad, I took it as my personal assignment to cheer them up. If a partner was stressed, I scrambled to remove obstacles from their path. If a colleague dropped a ball, I caught it before it hit the ground, usually without them even noticing.

I moved through life like a frantic emotional mechanic. I walked into rooms scanning for leaks, cracks, and squeaky wheels, ready to patch them up with my own energy.

I told myself I was being helpful. I told myself I was being "good."

But if I am honest, I wasn't just being helpful. I was anxious. I believed that if I could just make everyone around me happy and stable, then I would finally be allowed to relax. I was trying to create a calm environment for myself by micromanaging the emotions of everyone else.

The Heavy Backpack

Imagine you are hiking up a mountain. You have your own backpack to carry, filled with your own worries, dreams, and responsibilities. It is heavy, but it is yours.

Then you see someone struggling with their pack, so you say, "Here, let me take that." You see another person stumbling, so you grab their pack too.

Pretty soon, you are carrying three backpacks. You are sweating, your back is breaking, and you are resentful. You think, *"Why is everyone walking so freely while I am struggling?"*

The answer is uncomfortable: You are struggling because you stole their struggle.

When we rush to fix people, we often steal their backpacks. We are taking away their agency. We are taking away the weight they need to carry to become stronger.

The Theft of Growth

This was the hardest realization for me: Fixing is not always an act of love. Sometimes, it is a theft of growth.

- When you fix a mistake for a junior employee before they see the consequences, you rob them of the lesson that would make them a better professional.
- When you frantically entertain a bored child, you rob them of the creativity that comes from boredom.

- When you rush to soothe a friend's anger, you rob them of the chance to process their own emotions.

People need to struggle sometimes. They need to sit in the discomfort of their own choices. It is the only way any of us learn resilience. By stepping in too early, we aren't saving them; we are disabling them.

Resigning from the Role

So, how do we stop? How do we resign from a job we've held for decades?

We start by learning the difference between supporting and carrying.

- Carrying is doing it for them.
- Supporting is standing next to them while they do it.

Carrying says: *"Give it to me, I'll handle it."* Supporting says: *"That looks really heavy. I believe you are strong enough to handle it, and I'm right here if you need to talk."*

It feels unnatural at first. When you see a problem, your hands will twitch. You will want to jump in. You will feel a spike of anxiety thinking, *"If I don't fix this, it will all fall apart."*

Let it fall apart. Or, more likely, watch with amazement as it *doesn't* fall apart. Watch as the people around you figure it out. Watch as they step up because you finally step back.

The Peace of "Not My Problem"

There is a mantra I use now when I feel the urge to over-function. I repeat to myself: *"I am not the General Manager of the Universe."*

I am not responsible for the weather. I am not responsible for other people's moods. I am not responsible for the outcome of other people's choices.

When you hand back the backpacks you were never meant to carry, you suddenly stand taller. Your shoulders drop. You have energy for your own climb.

And the most beautiful part is when you stop trying to fix people, you give them the dignity of being their own heroes. You allow them to be adults, and you allow yourself to finally, truly, just be a friend.

Chapter 4
The Illusion of Control

(*Retiring the General Manager*)

Many of us hold a secret, superstitious belief that we rarely say out loud: *"If I worry about it enough, I can stop it from happening."*

We treat worry like a magical talisman. We think that if we obsess over our children's future, or our partner's health, or the economy, we are somehow contributing to the solution. We believe that our anxiety is a form of labor.

If we stop worrying, even for a moment, we feel reckless. We feel like a pilot taking their hands off the controls of a plane. We think, *"If I stop stressing, the plane will crash."*

However, here is the hard, liberating truth: You are not flying the plane. You are a passenger, and your white-knuckled grip on the armrest is not keeping the aircraft in the sky; aerodynamics is.

The Job You Never Applied For

Somewhere along the line perhaps when you became a parent, or a manager, or a wife, you accidentally accepted a promotion. You became the General Manager of the Universe.

The job description is impossible. You are in charge of:

- The weather.
- The traffic.
- Other people's moods.
- The stock market.
- Your adult child's romantic choices.
- The outcome of a medical test.

The pay is terrible (zero dollars); the benefits are non-existent (insomnia, high blood pressure, irritability), and the worst part? You are failing at the job.

You are failing because the job is a lie. You cannot manage the universe. You can barely manage your own hydration.

The shedding phase of life involves handing in your resignation letter. It involves looking at the chaos of the world and admitting: *"I am too small to fix this."*

The Hula Hoop of Control

To understand what you can actually control, I want you to visualize a Hula Hoop.

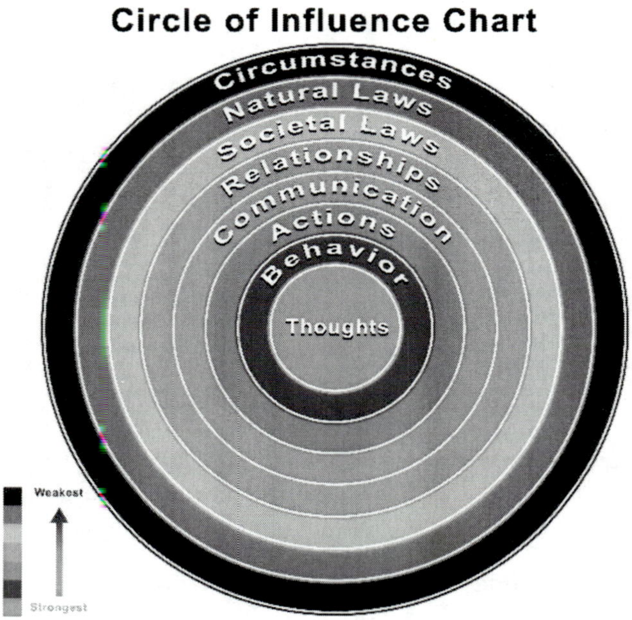

Shutterstock

Imagine placing a Hula Hoop on the ground and standing inside it.

- **Inside the Hoop:** Everything inside this circle is yours. It is your property. You have absolute authority here.
    - Your words.
    - Your actions.

  - Your boundaries.
  - Your integrity.
  - What you eat for breakfast.
  - How you respond to a crisis.
- **Outside the Hoop:** Everything outside the circle belongs to the Universe (or God, or Fate, or simply Reality).
  - What other people think of you.
  - What other people do.
  - Whether it rains.
  - Whether you get the job after the interview.
  - Whether your body heals or doesn't.

Anxiety happens when you step out of your hoop.

When you are trying to script your husband's conversation with his boss, you are out of your hoop. When you are lying awake at 3 AM replaying a mistake your daughter made, you are out of your hoop.

You are trespassing in reality.

The practice of the "Exhale" is simply looking down at your feet and checking: *"Am I in my hoop?"* If the answer is no, step back in.

Focus on your reaction, your breathing, your next step; that is where your power lives.

Care vs. Control

The hardest place to let go of control is with the people we love.

We convince ourselves that our micromanaging is love. We say, *"I just want what's best for them!"*, but there is a distinct line between Care and Control.

- Care is offering resources. It is saying, *"I love you, I am here for you, and I believe in you."*
- Control is demanding an outcome. It is saying, *"You must do it this way, or I will be anxious/angry."*

Control is actually a form of distrust. When we try to steer someone else's life, we are telling them: *"I don't trust you to handle your own journey. I don't trust you to survive your own mistakes."*

Dropping the illusion of control is the ultimate act of respect. It grants the people you love the dignity of their own path including their own potholes.

The Sweetness of Surrender

'Surrender" is a scary word. In war, it means you have lost. It means you are weak.

However, in life, surrender means you are wise.

Surrender does not mean giving up. It does not mean lying down and letting a truck run over you. Surrender means you stop fighting gravity.

It means you look at the reality of the moment, the diagnosis, the breakup, the rainstorm and you say:

"Okay. This is happening. I don't like it, but I acknowledge it is happening."

When you stop wasting your energy trying to change reality, you suddenly have a massive amount of energy available to navigate reality.

The Sky Stays Up

Try this experiment today.

Pick one thing you are worried about, something outside your Hula Hoop. Give yourself permission to stop holding it up for just one hour.

Tell yourself: *"For the next hour, I am going to assume the universe can handle this without my mental supervision."*

Exhale. Drop your shoulders.

Notice that the world keeps spinning. Notice that the sun keeps shining. Notice that the sky stays up, all by itself.

You were never holding it up. You were just exhausting yourself reaching for the ceiling.

Put your arms down. Rest. The universe has got this.

Chapter 5
Dropping the Rope
(Ending the Power Struggle)

Have you ever been in a tug-of-war?

Visualize it for a moment. You are holding a rough, heavy rope. Your muscles are burning. Your hands are blistered and raw. You are digging your heels into the mud, sweating, panting, determined not to be dragged across the line.

On the other side of the rope is the antagonist of your current story.

Maybe it is your ex-partner. Maybe it is a stubborn parent. Maybe it is a difficult boss, or a sibling who knows exactly how to get under your skin.

They are pulling just as hard as you are.

You tell yourself: *"I just have to pull harder. If I explain it one more time... if I send one more text... if I scream a little louder... I will win. I will pull them over to my side, and they will finally see things from my perspective."*

But the truth is, you have been pulling for five years. Or ten. Or twenty. Nobody has moved an inch. All that has happened is that your hands are bleeding.

The realization of the "Exhale" is simple but radical: The only way to win a tug-of-war is to drop the rope.

The Physics of Conflict

We tend to think that a fight is something happening *to* us but physics tells us otherwise. Tension requires resistance.

If you are pulling and the other person lets go, you fall backward. If they are pulling and *you* let go, they fall backward.

The struggle only exists because you are still holding on.

You are holding on because you think you are fighting for the Truth. You think you are fighting for Justice but really, you are fighting for Validation. You are waiting for them to say the magic words: *"You were right. I was wrong. I am sorry."*

I have to be the one to tell you: They are never going to say it.

And even if they did, it wouldn't fix the years you lost standing in the mud.

The Hook (Why We Don't Let Go)

Why is it so hard to drop the rope? Because the rope has a hook in it, and that hook is usually lodged in our ego.

- The Hook of "Being Right": You know you are logical. You have the receipts. You have the facts. It feels insane to let them "get away" with being wrong.

- The Hook of "The Last Word": We are obsessed with the mic drop. We want to send that final, perfect email that leaves them speechless.
- The Hook of "Fixing Them": We think, *"If I just love them enough/argue enough/explain enough, they will change."*

But here is the hard pill to swallow: You cannot reason a person out of a position they didn't reason themselves into.

If someone is committed to misunderstanding you, your explanation is not a bridge; it is just more rope.

Identifying the Bait

People who love a power struggle are master fishermen. They know exactly what bait to put on the hook to get you to pick the rope back up.

- The bait might be a guilt trip: *"I guess you just don't care about the family."*
- The bait might be an accusation: *"You're being crazy."*
- The bait might be false helplessness: *"I just don't understand why you're mad."*

The old you would bite. You would snap, *"I am NOT crazy!"* and grab the rope with both hands to prove your sanity.

The new you sees the bait, recognizes it for what it is, and keeps walking.

The Face-Plant

What happens when you finally drop the rope?

The other person will likely face-plant.

They are pulling with all their might, expecting your resistance to hold them up. When you let go, they lose their balance. They might get angry. They might get louder. They might try to provoke you more intensely because they are confused. They need your resistance to fuel their drama.

They will say: "Why aren't you answering me?" *You will say:* Nothing. Or, "I'm not having this conversation anymore."

Let them stumble. Let them sit in the mud with the slack rope in their hands. It is not your job to catch them.

What You Get in Return

You might worry that dropping the rope means you are "weak" or that you "lost."

However, look at your hands. When you are holding the rope, your hands are full. You cannot pick up anything else. You cannot hold a coffee. You cannot hold a book. You cannot hold your child's hand. You cannot hold your own peace.

When you drop the rope, your hands are empty, and because they are empty, they are free.

You get your energy back. The energy you used to spend drafting mental arguments in the shower. You get to keep that now. You can use it to create art, to build a business, or simply to sleep.

The Walk Away

Dropping the rope is not a loud event. You don't throw it down and scream, *"I surrender!"*

It is a quiet, internal shift. It is the moment you realize that your peace is more important than your point.

It is the moment you decide to stop engaging with the chaos. You unclench your fingers. You turn your back on the mud pit, and you walk away, leaving them to argue with the air.

You didn't lose. You just exited the game, and that … is the ultimate victory.

Chapter 6
The Empty Chair

There is a specific kind of loneliness that comes not from being alone, but from being with people who no longer know the person you have become.

You sit at dinner with old friends, or you visit family, or you attend the same weekly meeting you've gone to for years. They are telling the same jokes. They are complaining about the same problems. The dynamic is exactly the way it has always been.

But you are different. You changed.

You feel a little bit like a ghost in your own life. You are smiling and nodding, but inside, you feel a strange friction. You realize you are wearing an old version of yourself like a tight coat, just to fit in with the people around you.

This brings us to one of the most painful realizations of the exhale: When you grow, you will inevitably outgrow people.

The Myth of "Forever"

We are taught from a young age that the definition of a "successful" relationship, whether it's a marriage, a friendship, or a partnership is *longevity*. We believe that if a friendship fades, something went wrong. We think someone is to blame.

However, people are not static monuments. We are rivers. We are constantly moving, changing, and reshaping our banks.

It is a statistical miracle that two people would change in the exact same direction, at the exact same speed, for fifty years. Sometimes it happens, and it is beautiful, but often, it does not.

To outgrow a relationship is not a betrayal. It is physics.

As you shed your old patterns (the need to please, the need to fix, the need to perform), you change your frequency. The people who were attracted to your old patterns may not know how to connect with your new peace.

The Empty Chair is Not a Tragedy

So, relationships drift. Calls get shorter. Invites get declined.

Then, you look around your metaphorical dinner table, and you see an empty chair where a person used to be.

The old you would panic. The old you would chase them. You would text: *"Are you mad at me? What did I do?"* You would try to shrink yourself back down to size just to keep the chair filled.

But the "After" version of you, the one who is realigning, understands something vital: An empty chair is better than a forced conversation.

You learn to look at that empty space not with bitterness, but with gratitude. You can look at the space and say, *"Thank you for the season we shared. Thank you for what you taught me, and I wish you well on your own path."*

Seasonal Travelers

Think of your life as a long train ride.

Some people get on the train at the very first station and stay until the very end. These are rare and precious. Some people get on for just three stops. They sit next to you, you laugh, you share a sandwich, and then they get off at their station. Some people are there for the bumpy parts of the track, and some are there for the scenic route.

If you try to bar the doors and force everyone to stay on your train forever, you create a hostage situation, not a community.

Allowing people to get off at their station is an act of love. It respects their journey, and it respects yours.

The Space for What's Next

There is a final, secret benefit to the empty chair.

Nature hates a vacuum. When you clear the space of relationships that make you feel small, drained, or unseen, you create a vacuum, and the universe rushes to fill that space with things that match who you are *now*.

You cannot meet the people who will love your new self until you stop clinging to the people who only loved your old self.

So, don't be afraid of the shrinking circle. A small circle of truth is infinitely better than a large crowd of pretense. Let the chairs be empty for a while. Enjoy the legroom.

Part II

The Realignment

(The Quiet Room)

(Navigating the Void and Finding Intuition)

There is a terrifying gap between "no longer" and "not yet."

It happens after you have shed the old ways (Part I), but before you have fully figured out the new ways. I call this The Hallway.

Most people panic here.

When you stop over-functioning, when you fire the committee of voices in your head, and when you stop performing for an audience, the silence can be deafening. You feel untethered. You feel messy, like a caterpillar dissolving into soup before it becomes a butterfly.

In this section, we will learn to stand in that Hallway without rushing to the exit.

We are going to confront the "Great Unlearning," stripping away the scripts that told you productivity was your only worth. We are going to turn on your "Internal GPS" so you can stop asking strangers for directions to your own life. We are going to learn the difference between anxiety and intuition.

Perhaps most importantly, we are going to learn how to date ourselves. We are going to learn how to treat our own minds not as a chaotic workspace, but as a luxury suite.

This is not a passive waiting room. This is active soil. Just because a seed is underground doesn't mean nothing is happening. It is realigning. It is gathering strength.

Welcome to the quiet. You are safe here.

Chapter 7
The Hallway
(The Liminal Space)

There is a concept in storytelling and psychology called “Liminal Space." It comes from the Latin word *limen*, which means "threshold."

It is the space between "no longer" and "not yet."

- You have let go of the old job, but you haven't found the new calling.
- You have ended the relationship, but you haven't healed enough to date.
- You have stopped people-pleasing (the "Nice Girl" is dead), but you don't yet know who you are when you aren't performing.

This space feels like a long, dark hallway between two doors.

You have shut the door behind you, and you can’t go back but the door in front of you is still closed. You are standing in the dark, waiting for a handle to turn.

The Panic of the Void

The Hallway is terrifying because it feels empty.

Our culture hates emptiness. We are obsessed with momentum. We ask each other, *"What's next? What are you working on? Who are you seeing?"*

When you are in the Hallway, you have no answers. You feel like a ghost in your own life. You feel untethered.

The instinct is to panic. We think, *"I've made a mistake. I shouldn't have let go. At least the old room had furniture in it, even if I hated the furniture. At least I knew where to sit."*

This is where most people break. They turn around and pound on the locked door of their past, begging to be let back in, or they kick down the future door prematurely, forcing a solution that isn't ready.

The Trapeze Artist

I want you to imagine a trapeze artist high up in the circus tent.

She is swinging on the first bar. This is your old life. It is solid. You have a grip on it.

Then, she sees the second bar swinging toward her. This is your new life.

To get from one to the other, there is a terrifying requirement: She must let go of the first bar before she can catch the second.

She must float in mid-air. She must be supported by nothing but momentum and trust.

The Hallway is that moment in mid-air.

You are flying through the void. You aren't holding anything. It feels like falling, but it is actually *flying*. If you refuse to let go of the first bar until you have a firm grip on the second, you will never move. You will just hang there until your muscles give out.

Don't Decorate the Hallway

Because the Hallway is uncomfortable, we try to make it comfortable. We try to live there.

- We rush into a "rebound" relationship because sleeping alone is too quiet.
- We take a job we know we hate just to have a title on LinkedIn.
- We fill our schedule with "busy work" so we don't have to hear our own thoughts.

We are trying to hang pictures on the walls of a hallway. We are trying to put a sofa in the transit zone.

Stop it. Do not decorate the Hallway.

It is not meant to be a home. It is meant to be a passage. If you fill it with clutter to distract yourself from the anxiety, you block the path to the door at the end. You must be willing to stand in the emptiness.

Caterpillar Soup (The Science of Change)

Nature gives us the perfect blueprint for this.

We all know the story of the caterpillar and the butterfly, but do you know what actually happens inside the cocoon?

The caterpillar does not just sprout wings, that is a fairy tale.

In reality, the caterpillar digests itself. It releases enzymes that dissolve its entire body into a unrecognizable goo. It becomes "caterpillar soup."

If you cut open a cocoon halfway through the process, you wouldn't see a half-caterpillar, half-butterfly. You would see a mess.

However, inside that soup, there are things called "imaginal cells." These cells hold the blueprint of the butterfly. They use the protein of the dissolved caterpillar to build new wings, new eyes, the new life.

The Hallway is the Soup Phase.

You feel like you are falling apart. You feel like a mess. You feel like you have lost your structure. Good. That means it is working. You are dissolving the old identity so the new one can be built. You cannot keep the caterpillar body and have the butterfly wings.

You must become the soup first.

Active Waiting

So, what do you do in the Hallway?

If you can't go back and you can't go forward, what is the task?

The task is Active Waiting.

Passive waiting is staring at the clock, bored and resentful. Active waiting is gestation. It is rest. It is listening.

- You sleep more.
- You journal.
- You walk.
- You say "No" to things that don't feel like "Yes."
- You pay attention to what sparks your interest, even if it's small.

You trust that the door will open. You trust that the imaginal cells are doing their work. You trust that you don't need to force the butterfly out of the cocoon. If you force it, its wings will be shriveled and useless.

The Door Will Open

One day, the door at the end of the Hallway will crack open.

It might be a chance meeting. It might be a sudden idea. It might be a feeling of "Oh, I'm ready now."

It won't happen on your schedule. It will happen on your soul's schedule.

Until then, stand tall in the dark.

Don't rush. Don't panic.

And for the love of God, don't try to decorate.

Just breathe. You are on your way.

Chapter 8
The Great Unlearning

Realignment is rarely about learning new things. We are obsessed with self-improvement; we want to learn a new language, learn to meditate, learn to be more productive.

However, the transformation of the second half of life is almost entirely about unlearning.

We are born as wild, authentic, specific creatures. Just look at a toddler. They know exactly what they like (strawberries). They know exactly what they hate (itchy socks). They scream when they are mad. They sleep when they are tired. They are entirely themselves.

But from the moment we can speak, we are handed a script.

- *"Be a good girl."*
- *"Don't be too loud."*
- *"Success looks like a corner office."*
- *"Beauty looks like a size 4."*
- *"Selfishness is a sin."*

By the time we are forty, we have memorized this script so well that we think it is our DNA. We think, *"I'm just a naturally helpful person,"* when in reality, you might just be a person who was trained to believe that your worth depends on your utility.

The Domestication of the Soul

The author Glennon Doyle talks about being "tamed." I like to think of it as domestication.

We were domesticated house cats who were convinced we were supposed to act like Golden Retrievers. We spent decades trying to bark, trying to fetch, trying to be eager to please, and we were exhausted, because deep down, we were feline. We wanted to nap in the sun and only come when called if we felt like it.

The "Unlearning" is the process of looking at your life and asking: "Is this who I am, or is this who I was told to be?"

The Identity Audit

This phase requires a brutal audit of your own personality. You have to look at the things you "are" and question their origin.

- Are you actually an introvert, or were you just silenced so often as a child that you learned it was safer to be quiet?
- Are you actually a perfectionist, or did you just learn early on that mistakes were met with anger, so you developed perfectionism as a shield?

- Do you actually love your career, or did you just choose it because your father said it was "sensible"?
- Do you actually like hiking, or do you just go because your partner likes it and you want to be "easy-going"?

This is disorienting. It can make you feel angry. You might feel grief for the years you spent acting out a role you didn't audition for. That is normal. Let the grief come.

The Three Big Lies We Must Unlearn

While everyone's script is different, there are three lies that almost all of us have to unlearn in our forties.

1. The Lie: "Productivity = Worth." We were taught that we have to "earn" our rest. We were taught that a day doing nothing is a wasted day.
    - *The Unlearning:* You are a human being, not a human doing. Your value is innate. You deserve to exist even if you produce nothing today.
2. The Lie: "Conflict is Dangerous." We were taught that rocking the boat is bad. We learned to swallow our truth to keep the peace.
    - *The Unlearning:* Conflict is not abuse. Conflict is simply two truths meeting. You can survive someone being mad at you. The boat can rock without sinking.
3. The Lie: "I Can Fix People." We were taught that if we love someone enough, we can save them.

- *The Unlearning:* You cannot save anyone. You can only love them. Their journey is their own.

The Archaeology of the Self

Think of this process not as construction, but as archaeology.

You are not building a "new you." You are digging for the "original you."

You are taking a delicate brush and sweeping away the layers of dirt, the layers of expectation, the layers of "shoulds."

Then underneath all that debris, you find something ancient. You find the girl who liked to paint before she was told art doesn't make money. You find the woman who loves silence. You find the person who has a loud laugh and a messy heart.

Dealing with the Void

When you start unlearning, you might feel sudden emptiness.

If you stop being the "Helper," what are you? If you stop being the "Achiever," what are you?

This void scares people. They think, *"If I peel away all the layers of the onion, there will be nothing left."*

Hold on, that is the fear talking.

When you peel away the layers of the onion, you don't find nothing. You find the seed.

You find the core essence that has been waiting there for forty years, tapping its foot, waiting for you to come back home.

The Return to Wildness

The goal of the Great Unlearning is to become feral again.

Not in a "running around the woods naked" way (unless you want to), but in a spiritual way. To be feral is to be undomesticated. It is to trust your own hunger. It is to trust your own fatigue. It is to trust your own instincts over the commands of a master.

It is terrifying to drop the script. You might forget your lines. You might stand on stage in silence.

But eventually, a new voice will come out of your throat. It might be rusty. It might be shaky, but it will be yours….and that is the only voice worth listening to.

Chapter 9
The Luxury of a Quiet Mind

I used to be addicted to chaos. I didn't know it at the time, of course. I called it "passion."

I called it "hustle." I called it "living life to the fullest."

If my schedule wasn't packed back-to-back, I would feel lazy. If my relationships didn't have high highs and dramatic lows, I felt bored. I treated my nervous system like a roller coaster, believing that the adrenaline of stress was the same thing as the energy of life.

I was terrified of silence. Silence felt empty. Silence felt like the waiting room where you sit before real life begins.

But eventually, the roller coaster stops being fun. It just makes you nauseous.

The Badge of Busy

We live in a culture that worships exhaustion.

When you run into an old friend and ask, *"How are you?"*, what is the standard answer? *"Oh, I'm so busy. Crazy busy."*

We say it with a sigh, but there is a hidden pride in it. We wear our burnout like a badge of honor. We mistakenly believe that if we are busy, we are important. If we are exhausted, we must be doing a good job.

However, there is a difference between being busy and being effective, and there is a massive difference between having a full schedule and having a full life.

The realization that changed me was this: Busyness is often a form of laziness. It is lazy thinking and indiscriminate action. It is easier to say "yes" to everything and run around like a headless chicken than it is to do the hard work of saying "no" and prioritizing what matters.

The Withdrawal from Drama

When you first step away from the noise, when you stop chasing dramatic relationships, when you stop over-scheduling your weekends, when you stop scrolling until your eyes burn, it feels uncomfortable.

It feels like chemical withdrawal, and in a way, it is.

Your body is used to the hits of dopamine and cortisol that come from stress and drama. You sit in a quiet room on a Tuesday evening with nothing urgent to do, and your brain starts to itch. You think, *"I should be doing something. I should be fixing something. I should be worried about something."*

We are so accustomed to the hum of anxiety that when it stops, we think something is wrong. We mistake peace for boredom.

Redefining "Boring"

There comes a moment when you realize that "boring" is actually the most underrated word in the English language.

To a chaotic mind, a predictable day is a nightmare. To a healed mind, a predictable day is a sanctuary.

I have learned to love the "boring" things. The coffee that tastes the same every morning. The friend who doesn't bring drama, just steady presence. The evening where the biggest event is watching the sun go down.

This isn't settling. This is refining your palate.

Think of it like food.

A child loves sugary, neon-colored candy that explodes in their mouth, but as you mature, you learn to appreciate the subtle bitterness of dark chocolate or the complex quiet of a good tea. Your soul is learning to appreciate the subtle, rich flavor of tranquility.

You stop craving the fireworks of external validation, and you start craving the fireplace of internal warmth.

The Productivity Trap

The hardest hurdle to clearing your mind is the guilt.

We are trained to be "Human Doings" rather than "Human Beings." If we sit on the porch for twenty minutes without a book, a phone, or a task, we feel like we are sinning against capitalism.

"I'm wasting time," the voice in your head whispers.

However, you are not a machine. You are a garden. A garden does not bloom all year round. It has seasons of dormancy. It rests. It is in the resting that the roots grow deep.

When you allow your mind to be quiet, you are not wasting time; you are composting. You are letting your experiences settle, decomposing the stress, and turning it into wisdom.

Peace is the New Luxury

We live in a world that sells us luxury in the form of things; handbags, cars, vacations, but the true luxury of our time is not something you can buy.

The ultimate luxury is a quiet mind.

- To be able to sit in traffic and not feel your blood pressure rise. That is wealth.
- To receive a stressful email and not let it ruin your dinner. That is power.
- To lay your head on the pillow at night and not have a committee meeting in your brain. That is success.

This luxury is available to the CEO and the student, the mother and the artist. It costs nothing in money, but it costs everything in discipline. It requires the discipline to guard your mind as fiercely as you would guard your home.

The Static Clears

When you finally allow your mind to quiet down, a strange thing happens. You can hear yourself think.

For years, the voice of my intuition was drowned out by the static of my anxiety. I couldn't hear what I really wanted because I was too busy listening to what everyone else wanted from me, but in the quiet, the static clears. You start to remember who you were before the world told you who to be. You make decisions not out of fear, but out of knowing.

So, if you find yourself sitting in a quiet moment today, resist the urge to fill it. Don't pick up your phone. Don't turn on the TV. Don't look for a problem to solve.

Just sit there. Soak in the luxury of having nothing to do and nowhere to be. You have earned this silence.

Chapter 10
Good Enough is Perfect

There is a tyrant that lives in the minds of many of us. It is the voice of Perfectionism.

For years, I thought perfectionism was a virtue. I thought it meant I had high standards. I thought it meant I cared about quality. I wore my perfectionism like a badge of honor in job interviews and dinner parties.

Lady, I was wrong!

Perfectionism is not the pursuit of excellence. Perfectionism is the pursuit of safety.

My "if-then-else" statements will start again but bear with me.

We convince ourselves that if we are perfect, if we are the perfect mother, the perfect employee, the perfect partner then we will be beyond reproach. We think that if we do everything perfectly, then pain cannot touch us. Criticism cannot touch us.

We are building a fortress out of A-pluses, clean houses, and perfectly edited photos, but the problem with a fortress is that while it keeps the bad stuff out, it also keeps the good stuff out. You cannot let love in if you are standing guard at the gate, terrified of making a mistake.

The Law of Diminishing Returns

If you look at this logically, perfectionism is actually a terrible investment.

In economics, there is a concept called the "Law of Diminishing Returns." It states that after a certain point, adding more effort yields smaller and smaller results.

Think about writing an email.

- Writing the draft takes 5 minutes. It conveys the message. It is 90% good.
- Then you spend 15 more minutes re-reading it, changing a comma, worrying about the tone, and deleting a sentence.
- You just spent 300% more time making the email 1% better.

We do this with everything. We scrub the house before the guests arrive, not to make them comfortable, but to prove we have control. We over-prepare for the meeting not to be useful, but to be unimpeachable.

The realization that set me free was this: The last 10% of effort usually costs 90% of your peace.

Is that last 10% really worth your sanity? Is it worth your sleep? Usually, the answer is no.

The 80% Rule

To combat the tyrant, I adopted the "80% Rule."

- A house that is 80% clean is a lovely, hygienic place to live. A house that is 100% clean is a museum where no one can relax.
- A project that is 80% perfect and finished is infinitely better than a project that is 100% perfect and sits in your drawer forever.
- A dinner party with 80% good food and a relaxed host is memorable. A dinner party with 100% gourmet food and a stressed-out host is uncomfortable.

When you aim for "Good Enough," you are not being lazy. You are being efficient. You are saving your energy for the things that actually matter; connections, rest, and joy.

The Edited Life vs. The Lived Life

We live in an age of curation. We have tools in our pockets that allow us to filter our faces, edit our captions, and crop out the messy corners of our rooms.

This has trained us to believe that our lives should look like magazines, but a magazine is a staged set.

A life is a messy, breathing, chaotic ecosystem.

When you release the need to be perfect, you stop performing for an invisible audience.

- You leave the house without makeup because you want to feel the sun on your face, not because you gave up.
- You invite friends over when there are dishes in the sink because you want their company more than you want their approval.
- You admit you don't know the answer to a question because you are confident enough to be a learner.

Embracing the Flaw (Kintsugi)

There is a Japanese art form called *Kintsugi*, where broken pottery is repaired with gold lacquer. Instead of hiding the cracks, they highlight them. The break is what makes the object beautiful and unique.

We need to apply *Kintsugi* to our lives.

The stumble in your career? That gave you resilience.

The relationship that failed? That taught you what you really need.

The years you spent lost? That gave you the map you have now.

Your flaws are not failures. They are the gold lacquer. They are evidence that you have lived, tried, and survived.

The Invitation

So, I invite you to lower the bar.

Aim for "B-minus" work in areas that don't matter, so you can save your "A-plus" energy for the things that truly bring you joy.

Resign from the cult of perfection. Take off the armor.

The air is much easier to breathe down here in the messy, beautiful reality of "Good Enough."

Chapter 11
The Internal GPS
(Trusting Intuition)

One of the greatest casualties of the first half of life is our Intuition.

We aren't born doubting ourselves. A toddler knows exactly what they want. They know when they are hungry. They know when they like someone. They know when they want to leave. They are fully inhabited.

But then, the training begins.

- We are told to hug the relative we are afraid of. (Lesson: *Ignore your gut.*)
- We are told to finish the food on our plate even though we are full. (Lesson: *Ignore your body.*)
- We are told that our anger is "unbecoming." (Lesson: *Your emotions are wrong.*)

Slowly, we learn to mute the internal voice. We replace our Internal GPS with an external polling system.

By the time we are forty, we treat our lives like a democracy. We poll a committee every time we need to make a move.

- *"Do you think I should take the job?"*
- *"Do you think this dress is too young for me?"*
- *"Do you think I should stay in this marriage?"*

We ask the internet. We ask our friends. We ask experts. We are desperate for someone else to give us the permission slip to live our own lives.

Firing the Committee

The Realignment requires a hostile takeover of your own mind. It is time to Fire the Committee.

Imagine a boardroom table in your head. Sitting around it are your mother, your father, your high school bully, your boss, and that judgmental neighbor. Every time you have a decision to make, you look at them for approval.

You need to walk into that room and say: *"Thank you for your service. You are all dismissed."*

Clear the room. Sit at the head of the table.

You are the world's leading expert on **You**. The CEO might know business, but he doesn't know your soul. The doctor might know medicine, but she doesn't know your pain. Your mother might know her life, but she doesn't know yours.

The Signal and the Static

The reason we can't hear our intuition is because the signal is buried under static.

The static is the "Shoulds."

- *I should be grateful.*

- *I should be working harder.*
- *I should be nicer.*

The Intuition is the quiet voice underneath that says: *"This isn't working."*

Intuition is rarely loud. It doesn't scream. It doesn't use a PowerPoint presentation to convince you. It is a humble, steady knowing. It is the click of a lock falling into place.

Anxiety vs. Intuition (How to Tell the Difference)

The biggest question I get is: *"How do I know if it's my Intuition or just my Fear?"*

They can feel similar, both can make your stomach drop, but they have very different signatures.

1. The Voice
    - Anxiety is frantic. It talks fast. It sounds like a spinning hamster wheel. It asks, "What if?" a thousand times. *"What if you quit and go broke? What if everyone laughs? What if you fail?"*
    - Intuition is calm. It is flat. It doesn't ask; it states. *"It is time to go." "He is not the one." "Don't get in that car."*
2. The Location
    - Anxiety lives in the head. It is a mental swirl.
    - Intuition lives in the body. It is a dropping sensation in the gut, or a heaviness in the chest, or a sudden ability to breathe freely.

3. The Emotional Aftermath
    - Anxiety feels draining.
    - Intuition, even when it tells you something hard (like "Leave the job"), brings a strange sense of relief. It feels like the truth.

The Body Compass

Your body is a lie detector test that you cannot cheat.

The mind can rationalize anything. The mind can say, *"He checks all the boxes, he has a good job, he's nice...",* but the body knows.

We need to re-learn how to read the Body Compass.

- The "No" Signal: Constriction. Tightness in the jaw. Holding your breath. A feeling of shrinking. Nausea. Dread.
- The "Yes" Signal: Expansion. Shoulders dropping. Deep, involuntary exhales. A feeling of leaning in. Warmth.

During the Realignment, stop asking *"What do I think?"* and start asking *"What does my body do when I think about this option?"*

If you think about accepting that invitation and your body feels like it weighs 500 pounds... that is a No. I don't care how "polite" it would be to go. Your body has spoken.

Low Stakes Training

If you haven't used your GPS in twenty years, you can't start by navigating a cross-country trip. You have to start with a trip to the grocery store.

You need to practice on Low Stakes Decisions.

- Look at a menu. Don't ask what everyone else is having. Don't ask what is "healthy." Ask your gut: *What do I want?* And order it.
- Drive home a different way just because you 'feel like it."
- Cancel plans because you are tired and notice that the world didn't end.

Every time you listen to that quiet nudge and act on it, you strengthen the signal. You are building trust with yourself.

The Cost of overriding the GPS

We think that ignoring our intuition is the "safe" choice. It keeps the peace. It keeps us employed.

However, the cost is astronomical. When you override your GPS for years, you end up with a life that looks right on paper but feels wrong in your bones.

You end up with resentment.

You end up with mystery illnesses because your body is screaming to be heard.

Trusting yourself is terrifying at first. You might make a mistake, but I would rather make a mistake that is mine than live a "perfect" life that belongs to someone else.

Chapter 12
Dating Yourself

There is a specific phrase that used to terrify me.

Three little words that felt like a public admission of failure:

"Table for one, please."

For years, I treated my own company like a waiting room. I wouldn't go to the new Italian restaurant unless I had a date. I wouldn't go to the cinema to see the movie I really wanted to see unless a friend agreed to go with me. I wouldn't buy the expensive flowers for the coffee table unless guests were coming over.

I was living my life on standby. I was waiting for other people to co-sign my joy. I was waiting for permission to live.

But here is the truth that changed everything: You are the longest relationship you will ever have.

People will come and go. Children grow up and leave. Friends move cities. Partners may drift or pass away.

But *you*? You are stuck with you. From your first breath to your last, you are the only person who will be there for every single second of the journey.

So, why do we treat ourselves like a stranger, or worse, like an afterthought?

Solitude is Not Loneliness

First, we have to clear up a major misunderstanding. We often confuse loneliness with solitude. They look the same from the outside, a person sitting alone in a room, but they feel completely different on the inside.

- Loneliness is the pain of being alone. It is the feeling that something is missing. It is a poverty of the self.
- Solitude is the glory of being alone. It is the feeling that everything is present. It is the richness of the self.

When you date yourself, you are moving from loneliness to solitude. You are learning that an empty room doesn't have to feel empty; it can feel spacious. It can feel full of potential.

The Art of the Solo Date

The first time I took myself on a proper date, it felt excruciating.

I went to a nice restaurant. I put on lipstick. I brought a book, but I promised myself I wouldn't hide behind it.

When I asked for a table for one, the host looked at me with what I interpreted as pity. When the waiter took away the second set of cutleries, I felt a phantom limb. I felt exposed. I had the overwhelming urge to pull out my phone and scroll through emails just to look "busy," to signal to the room: *I have friends! I am important! I am just here alone by accident!*

I resisted. I sat there. I looked at the menu. I ordered the wine I wanted, not the one everyone else agreed on. I ate slowly.

Then something amazing happened about halfway through the meal, the anxiety broke. It was replaced by a strange, quiet euphoria.

I realized I didn't have to make conversation. I didn't have to worry if the other person was enjoying their food. I didn't have to compromise. I was entirely blissfully free. I tasted my food more than I had in years. I noticed the music. I noticed *me*.

Stop Saving the Good China

How often do you save the "good stuff" for other people?

- You wear an old, stained T-shirt to sleep on, but wear the silk pajamas when a partner stays over.
- You eat leftovers standing over the sink but cook a three-course meal for a dinner party.
- You use the chipped mugs for your morning coffee, leaving the beautiful porcelain cups in the cabinet for "guests."

This behavior sends a powerful, subconscious message to your brain: *I am not worth the effort. I am only worth the effort when someone else is watching.*

Dating yourself means breaking the good china for a Tuesday night spaghetti dinner. It means buying an expensive candle and burning it while you fold laundry. It means treating yourself with the same romance, curiosity, and tenderness you would offer a new lover.

Be High Maintenance (For Yourself)

We are often told not to be "high maintenance.", but I want you to be high maintenance, for yourself.

Maintain your standards. Maintain your boundaries. Maintain your joy.

If you are "low maintenance" with yourself, you eventually become "high resentment" with others. You start expecting them to fill the cup that you refuse to fill yourself. You start thinking, *"Why doesn't anyone take me out? Why doesn't anyone buy me flowers?"*

When you date yourself, you buy the damn flowers. You take yourself to the beach. You fill your own cup so high that when you interact with others, you aren't looking to take; you are ready to overflow.

The Micro-Date

You might be thinking, *"I don't have time for dinner alone."* That's okay. Start with a micro-date.

- The Car Date: Arrive at your destination 10 minutes early. Don't go in. Just sit in the car, listen to your favorite song, and breathe. That is a date.

- The Coffee Date: Sit in the coffee shop for 15 minutes without your phone. Watch the steam rise from the cup. Taste the foam. That is a date.
- The Walking Date: Walk around the block, not for exercise, but just to look at the trees.

The Paradox of Connection

Here is the irony: *The better you get at being alone, the better you become at being with others.*

When you are terrified of being alone, you will cling to bad relationships because they are better than nothing. You will tolerate disrespect because you need a warm body to fill the silence.

However, when you love your own company, you become selective. You stop looking for people to complete you, and you start looking for people to complement you. You stop being a hungry beggar looking for scraps of attention, and you become a host inviting people to a banquet that is already full.

So, take yourself to the movies. Buy the ticket. Eat all the popcorn.

Go to the museum and stare at the one painting you like for twenty minutes and skip the rest.

Learn to be the love of your own life.

That way, if anyone else comes along, it's just a bonus.

And if they don't, you are still in excellent company.

Part III
The Softening
(Making Peace with the Life You Have)

The world tells us that as we age, we should become harder. We should "fight" aging. We should "lean in" to ambition. We should build walls to protect our assets.

However, the "Exhale" asks us to do the opposite: It asks us to soften.

This section is about making peace with reality. It is about looking at your body, not as a renovation project to be fixed, but as a beloved home to be honored. It is about looking at your past, not as a museum of regrets and "what ifs," but as the perfect path that led you here.

We will talk about shifting your ambition from a "Ladder" (where you climb alone) to a "Campfire" (where you gather others for warmth). We will talk about the "Council of Wise Women", finding the deep, 4 AM friendships that sustain us, and the difficult, liberating art of forgiveness.

We are moving from conquering to connecting. We are moving from competition to collaboration.

You have spent enough time at war with yourself.

Lay down your weapons.

It is time to return to the sandbox and remember what it feels like to play.

Chapter 13
The Body is a Home, Not a Project

For decades, I treated my body like a renovation project that was running behind schedule.

I looked in the mirror and saw a to-do list. Fix this. Tighten that. Hide this. Color that.

I treated my body like an unruly employee that needed to be disciplined into submission. I withheld food to punish it; I exercised to conquer it. I was a cruel landlord to my own skin.

I believed that if I could just get the "renovation" finished; if I could just hit that number on the scale or erase that line on my forehead, then I would finally be happy.

But in the exhale years, you realize: ** The renovation is never going to be finished. ** and more importantly, you realize that your body is not a house you are trying to flip for a profit. It is the house you live in.

The War on "Anti-Aging"

We are bombarded with the phrase "Anti-Aging." It is on every cream, every serum, every magazine cover.

Think about what that phrase actually means. To be "anti-aging" is to be "anti-living."

To age is to survive. To age is to have navigated the dangers of the world and stayed alive. Every wrinkle is a receipt of a smile, a squint against the sun, or a moment of deep thought. Every scar is a story of healing. To want to erase these things is to want to erase the evidence that you have existed.

I have stopped trying to look like a woman who hasn't lived. I want to look like a woman who has lived *well*.

The Shift from Object to Subject

In our twenties, we are often treated as "Objects"; things to be looked at. We derive our power from heads turning when we walk into a room.

In our forties and beyond, we become "Subjects"; the ones doing the looking.

There is a panic that sets in when you realize you are becoming "invisible" to the male gaze or the public eye. You walk into a room, and heads don't turn.

At first, this feels like a loss of power, but if you sit with it, you realize it is the ultimate freedom.

When you are no longer performing for an audience, you can finally be the director of the play. You are not here to be decorative. You are here to be effective. You are here to observe, to create, and to impact.

Thanking the Tenant

When you stop critiquing your body, you can finally start thanking it.

This body carried you through heartbreaks where you thought you'd die, but your heart kept beating. It healed from fevers. It walked you into job interviews when your knees were shaking. It birthed children (or ideas, or futures)

It has been your most loyal companion, even when you were speaking hateful things to it in the mirror.

So, let the belly be soft; it is protecting your organs. Let the joints creak; they have walked thousands of miles.

Treat your body like an old, beloved dog that has been by your side for fifteen years.

You don't kick the dog because it's moving slower, or its fur is greying. You give it a soft bed. You give it the good food. You offer it grace.

Chapter 14
The Heavy Suitcase
(The Art of Forgiveness)

For a long time, I thought forgiveness was a gift I gave to the person who hurt me.

I thought that if I forgave them, I was being weak. I thought I was saying, *"What you did was okay."* I thought I was letting them off the hook.

So, I held onto my anger. I nursed my grudge. I kept the timeline of their offenses perfectly organized in my mind, ready to present it as evidence in a court that was never going to convene.

I thought my anger was a shield. I thought it protected me from getting hurt again but actually, my anger wasn't a shield. It was a suitcase.

A heavy, lead-lined suitcase that I insisted on carrying everywhere I went.

- I took it on vacation to Bali, dragging it across the sand.
- I took it to dinner with friends, setting it on the empty chair next to me.

- I took it to bed, letting it take up the space where peace should be.

I was exhausted. My back was breaking.

And the person who hurt me? They were sleeping just fine. They weren't carrying the suitcase. I was.

The Acid in the Vessel

There is an old saying: *"Resentment is like drinking poison and waiting for the other person to die."*

It is biologically true. When you hold onto deep anger, your body stays in a state of high alert. Your cortisol spikes. Your jaw clenches. Your digestion slows. You are physically corroding your own vessel to punish someone who isn't even in the room.

The Softening phase of life requires us to realize that unforgiveness is a form of self-poisoning.

When you hate someone, you are tethered to them. You are emotionally handcuffed to the person who broke your heart. They are renting space in your head for free. They are eating your food. They are using your energy.

Forgiveness is not about them. It is about eviction.

The Debt Ledger (Stop Being the Accountant)

I want you to imagine that your anger is an accounting ledger. Every time this person hurt you, you wrote it down.

- *"They owe me an apology."*
- *"They owe me a childhood."*

- *"They owe me 10 years of my life."*

You are walking around clutching this ledger, waiting for them to pay up. You check the balance every day. You re-read the line items.

Forgiveness is the moment you realize: They cannot pay.

Maybe they are too broken to pay. Maybe they are too narcissistic to admit they owe you. Maybe they are dead.

Forgiveness is taking that ledger, stamping "DEBT CANCELLED" in big red ink, and burning the book. You aren't cancelling the debt because they paid you back. You are cancelling it because you are tired of being the “accountant”. You are tired of sitting in the debt collection office waiting for a check that is never coming.

You are choosing to be bankrupt of their apology so that you can be rich in your own peace.

Crucial Distinction: Forgiveness vs. Reconciliation

This is where most people get stuck. They think, *"If I forgive him, I have to have Sunday dinner with him."*

No. Absolutely not.

We must separate Forgiveness from Reconciliation.

- Forgiveness is an internal release. It happens in your heart. It is a solo act. It releases the bitterness so you can heal.
- Reconciliation is an external reunion. It happens in the real world. It requires *two* people. It

requires the offender to apologize, change behavior, and rebuild trust.

You can forgive someone and never speak to them again.

You can forgive your toxic parents and keep the door locked. You can forgive your ex *and* block their number. You can forgive the thief *and* call the police.

Forgiveness says, *"I wish you no harm."* Boundaries say, *"You are not allowed in my house."*

The Softening means you stop wishing for their destruction. You wish them well—way over there, far away from your life.

The Myth of "Closure"

We often wait for "closure."

We want one last conversation where they admit what they did but in the second half of life, we learn that closure is a myth.

You will likely never get the apology you deserve. They will likely never understand your pain. If you wait for them to validate your reality, you will wait forever.

Closure is something you give yourself.

Closure is deciding that the story ends here. You turn the page, not because the plot was resolved perfectly, but because you are bored with this chapter and you want to see what happens in the next one.

Dropping the Suitcase

How do you actually do it?

It is a practice. You might have to forgive them ten times a day. You wake up, remember the hurt, and pick up the suitcase. Then you catch yourself. You say, *"No. I am not carrying this today."* And you set it down.

At first, your hands will feel strange. They have been clenched for so long that they don't know how to be open. You might feel lighter, but also a little off-balance. That is normal.

Soon, you will realize that because your hands are empty, they are free to hold other things. You can hold the hand of someone who actually loves you. You can hold a book. You can hold your own heart.

Put it down. Walk away. Let them carry their own baggage. You have a mountain to climb, and you need to travel light.

Chapter 15
The Museum of Unlived Lives

There is a ghost that haunts many of us in the middle of life. It is the ghost of the life we didn't choose.

- The career we didn't pursue because it was "too risky."
- The partner we didn't marry.
- The city we didn't move to.
- The child we didn't have (or the one we did).

We look at our current reality with its dirty dishes, its routine boredom, and its inevitable frustrations, and we wonder, *"What if I had turned left instead of right?"*

We torture ourselves with the idea that there is a "Perfect Version" of our life running in a parallel universe, where we are richer, happier, thinner, and wiser.

The Myth of the Green Grass

To find peace, we have to visit the Museum of Unlived Lives, look at the exhibits, and then walk out.

We tend to hallucinate that the unchosen path is paved with gold. We imagine the "Artist Life" we didn't pick is full of romance and inspiration. We forget it is also full of poverty, rejection, and instability.

We imagine the "Single Life" we left behind is full of freedom and excitement. We forget it is also full of loneliness and dating apps.

Every choice comes with a tax. The tax of marriage is compromise. The tax of singleness is solitude. The tax of a career is stress. The tax of freedom is instability.

There is no tax-free life. The version of you in that parallel universe is struggling too, just with different problems.

The Dignity of Choice

Every choice is a killing. That sounds violent, but it is just the math of existence.

When you chose your partner, you killed the possibility of being with anyone else. When you chose your career, you killed the possibility of the others.

For the first half of life, we want to keep all doors open. We hate closing doors. We want to be "pure potential."

However, potential is just a fancy word for "nothing has happened yet."

To mourn your unlived lives is to disrespect the life you actually built.

This life, the one with the stained carpet and the difficult boss and the friend who calls you at 10 PM, is the only one that is *real*. It is solid. It is yours.

Watering the Concrete

Don't mourn the seeds that didn't grow. Water the garden you are standing in.

It is easy to love a fantasy life because a fantasy has no flaws.

It is hard to love a real life because it is messy, but the mess is where the magic is.

Make peace with your choices.

Stand in the center of your life, look around at the imperfect reality, and say: *"I chose this, and I will make it beautiful."*

Chapter 16
Campfire Ambition
(Redefining Success)

In our twenties and thirties, ambition has a very specific geometry. It looks like a Ladder.

It is vertical. It is solitary. It is about altitude.

We spend decades looking up at the shoes of the person above us, trying to grab the next rung. We are fueled by the desire for "More." More money, more status, more followers, a bigger title, a bigger house.

We believe that if we just climb high enough, we will finally reach a place where we feel safe and validated.

But for many of us, somewhere around 40 or 50, the climbing stops feeling like an adventure and starts feeling like a punishment. You look at the next rung; the promotion, the expansion, the bigger responsibility, and instead of excitement, you feel exhaustion. You look at the view from where you are and realize: *"It's kind of cold up here ... and I'm alone."*

This is usually the moment a woman panics. She thinks, *"I've lost my edge. I'm giving up. I'm becoming irrelevant."*

But you haven't lost your ambition. Your ambition has just changed shape. It stopped looking like a Ladder and started looking like a **Campfire**.

Vertical vs. Horizontal Ambition

Vertical Ambition (The Ladder) is about *height*. It is zero-sum. There is only room for one person at the top of the ladder. If I win, you lose. It requires you to be armored, competitive, and constantly moving.

Horizontal Ambition (The Campfire) is about *warmth*. It is communal. A fire grows brighter when more logs are added. There is room for everyone to sit around it. It requires you to be open, stationary, and connected.

The shift in the second half of life is realizing that you are done climbing. You are done trying to be "above" people. Now, you want to be with people.

"I Am Building a Fire"

This confuses the world. People are used to the Ladder. They will ask you:

- "W*hy didn't you apply for that VP role?"*
- *"Why are you downsizing your business?"*
- *"Why aren't yo*u hustling anymore?"

They assume that because you aren't climbing, you are falling.

You can look them in the eye and say: "I am not climbing anymore. I am building a fire."

I want to gather good people around me. I want to tell stories. I want to share resources. I want to create a space where people feel safe enough to take off their armor. I am no longer interested in being the most "impressive" person in the room. I am interested in being the warmest.

The Crisis of Relevance

The hardest part of leaving the Ladder is the fear of irrelevance. We have been taught that if we aren't "crushing it," we don't matter. If we aren't the star, we are nobody.

But the Campfire offers a new role: The Keeper of the Fire.

In ancient tribes, the most respected role wasn't just the hunter; it was the elder who kept the fire burning. The one who held the wisdom. The one who knew the history.

When you switch to Campfire Ambition, you become a connector. You become a mentor.

- You aren't trying to prove you are smarter than the junior employee; you are trying to help them succeed.
- You aren't trying to outshine your friends; you are trying to illuminate them.

You realize that your relevance doesn't come from being the loudest voice. It comes from being the safest harbor.

Fueling the Flame

The fuel for the Ladder is **Insecurity** (*I need to prove I am enough*). The fuel for the Campfire is Enoughness (*I know I am enough, so now I can rest and share*).

This is a massive shift in energy. Ladder energy is frantic, cortisol-fueled, and brittle. Campfire energy is steady, warm, and sustainable.

Ask yourself: What actually warms you now?

- Is it hitting a sales goal, or is it having a three-hour dinner with a friend where you both laugh until you cry?
- Is it buying a luxury car, or is it having the time to walk your dog in the morning without looking at your watch?

The Legacy of Warmth

When you die, nobody will care how high you climbed on the ladder. They won't care about your title or your net worth.

They will remember how they felt when they sat next to you. They will remember if you made them feel seen. They will remember if you offered them a seat by the fire when they were cold.

So, let the climbers climb. Let them race to the top of the lonely peak. You have work to do down here on the ground. Gather the wood. Strike the match. Call your people in.

It is time to build something that lasts.

Chapter 17
The Council of Wise Women
(Deepening Friendship)

When we are young, friendship is often about Activity.

We have "going out" friends. We have "work" friends. We have friends who are fun because they are loud, or because they know where the good parties are, or because our kids are on the same soccer team. Our social life is wide, frantic, and often superficial. It is based on Proximity and Fun.

But as we enter the softening years, our tolerance for superficiality hits zero.

You find yourself sitting at a loud dinner party, shouting over the music about weather or real estate, and you feel a physical ache in your chest. You think: *"I am too tired for this. I don't want to shout small talk. I want to whisper the truth."*

You don't want to go to a bar. You want to sit on a porch. You don't want 50 friends who know your job title. You want three friends who know your fear.

The Great Edit

This phase often begins with what I call The Great Edit.

It can be painful. You might find that relationships you've held for decades suddenly feel ill-fitting. The friend who only calls to gossip. The friend who competes with you. The friend who only talks about herself.

In your thirties, you tolerated them because you were building a network. In your forties, you release them because you are building a sanctuary.

This isn't malice. It is discernment. You realize you have limited energy. You stop collecting people and start selecting them. You realize that a small circle of truth is infinitely stronger than a large crowd of pretense.

The 4 AM Friend

We stop looking for "Happy Hour Friends" and start looking for "4 AM Friends."

A Happy Hour friend is there for the champagne toast. She is great when you are winning. A 4 AM friend is the one you can call when the world falls apart.

- She is the one who will sit on your floor and eat pizza while you cry, without trying to fix it.
- She is the one who sees your messy house and doesn't judge but instead starts loading the dishwasher.
- She is the one who knows the darkest thing about you and looks at you with more love, not less.

We need fewer people, but we need them to be heavier. We need them to have gravity.

The Council

I like to think of this inner circle as The Council.

In ancient times, the village would have a council of elders, women who had lived through the storms and gathered the wisdom. You need your own Council.

This isn't a formal club. It might be a group chat. It might be a weekly walk. It might be one woman who lives three states away. The Council is the place where you can take off your armor.

Everywhere else in your life; at work, with your kids, maybe even with your partner, you have to hold it together. You have to be the "General Manager." With the Council, you are allowed to fall apart. You are allowed to say, *"I don't know what I'm doing." "I'm terrified." "I made a mistake."*

The Council doesn't offer platitudes. They offer Witness. They say, *"I see you. I've been there. You will survive."*

From Competition to Collaboration

For a long time, women are trained to compete. We are taught that there is only one seat at the table. We check to see who is aging better, whose kids are smarter, whose husband is richer. We view other women as mirrors that show us our own flaws.

The Softening destroys competition.

You look at another woman and you don't see a rival. You see a fellow soldier. You see the lines on her face and you know they came from the same worry that gave you yours. You see her success and you don't feel jealous; you feel relief, because if she can do it, maybe you can too.

You realize that every woman is a library.

Instead of comparing yourself to her, you want to read her book.

- *"How did you survive the divorce?"*
- *"How did you handle the empty nest?"*
- *"How did you learn to be so brave?"*

We stop fighting each other and start teaching each other. We trade maps.

The Safety Net

There is a statistic that says loneliness is as deadly as smoking. As we age, our partners may pass. Our children will leave. Our careers will end.

What remains is the web of friendship we have woven.

If you have invested in the Council, if you have shown up, listened, told the truth, and been vulnerable, you will never be truly alone. You will have a safety net made of strong, soft hands, ready to catch you when you fall.

So, make the phone call. Send the text. Schedule the walk.

Prioritize your women. They are the water in the desert.

Chapter 18
Return to the Sandbox

Somewhere along the line, we decided that "fun" had to be "productive."

We don't just go for a run; we train for a 5K. We don't just cook; we try to master a soufflé for a dinner party. We don't just doodle; we take a certification course in graphic design. We don't just write; we try to get published.

We monetized our hobbies. We turned our joy into side hustles. We forgot how to be amateurs.

The Meaning of "Amateur"

The word "amateur" comes from the Latin word *amare*, which means "to love."

An amateur is not someone who is bad at something. An amateur is someone who does it for the love of it, not for the money, the status, or the applause.

We need to reclaim the spirit of the amateur.

When we are children, we play in the sandbox without worrying if we are building a "structurally sound" castle. We don't ask, *"Can I put this sandcastle on my resume?"* We just like the feel of the sand.

As adults, we are so terrified of looking foolish that we stop playing. We stiffen up. We become "Serious People."

The Joy of Being Bad at Something

I want to invite you to do something radical: Do something you are bad at, just because you like it.

- Sing off-key in the car. Who cares if you can't carry a tune? The vibration feels good in your chest.
- Paint a picture that looks like a smudge. You aren't trying to get into a gallery; you are trying to play with color.
- Dance in the kitchen with no rhythm.

When you allow yourself to be bad at something, you break the chains of perfectionism. You remind yourself that your worth is not tied to your output.

High Stakes vs. No Stakes

Your life is full of high stakes. Your job, your family, your finances, these require competence. You must be good at them.

That is why you need a "No Stakes" Zone.

You need a corner of your life where performance doesn't matter. You need a place where you can fail, and nobody dies.

This is not a waste of time. This is how you oil the gears of your soul. When you play, you remind yourself that you are not just a worker bee designed to produce honey. You are a butterfly designed to enjoy the flower.

Go buy cheap watercolors. Go hit the tennis ball over the fence.

Go be a disastrously happy amateur.

Part IV
The View from Living in the Sixth Sky

(Wisdom, Mortality, and Legacy)

When you are in the thick of the jungle, all you can see are the vines in front of your face. You are hacking away, worried about the snakes, worried about the path, worried about the traffic.

However, when you finally climb above the canopy, the geography changes.

The jungle is still there. The problems are still there; but *you* are different because you can see the whole landscape.

This brings us to the final phase of our journey: Perspective.

We are operating now from a higher altitude; what I call the "Sixth Sky."

From up here, we stop chasing the visible trophies of status and start collecting the invisible trophies of character.

In this section, we will face the "elephant in the room," our own mortality and find that it is not a source of fear, but a source of vibrant urgency. We will choose "The Second Innocence," rejecting lazy cynicism in favor of defiant hope.

Finally, we will talk about your legacy.

Not a statue made of stone, but the "Legacy of Ripples," the invisible, contagious energy of kindness that you leave behind in every room you enter.

You have shed the weight. You have found your center. You have softened your heart.

Now, look at the horizon.

It’s beautiful from here.

Chapter 19
Invisible Trophies

If you walked into my house ten years ago, you would have seen the visible evidence of my life. You might have seen diplomas on the wall, photos of smiling vacations, or a closet full of clothes that fit a specific mold.

We spend the first half of our lives chasing visible trophies.

We want the Title. The Salary.

The Ring. The House. The "Perfect" Family.

We want the things that other people can point to and say, *"Look, she made it. She is successful."* We collect these things like squirrels collecting nuts, hoping that if we have a big enough pile, we will feel safe. We hope that if we look successful on the outside, we will finally feel successful on the inside.

Then, a strange thing happens. You get the trophy. You get the promotion. You buy the house, and you stand in the middle of your "success" and feel a draft. You realize that external accolades cannot fill internal holes.

The applause dies down. The crowd goes home, and you are left with yourself.

This is the moment the search changes. You stop looking for things to put on a shelf, and you start looking for things to put in your soul.

The Real Achievements

Welcome to the concept of Invisible Trophies.

An Invisible Trophy is awarded for a victory that happens entirely inside your own chest. There is no ceremony. There is no raise. There is no Instagram post. In fact, often, nobody even knows if a battle took place.

But you know.

These are the trophies that actually build a life.

1. The Trophy of Restraint

You win this when someone says something cruel, ignorant, or baiting to you. The old you would have snapped back. The old you would have spent three days crafting a retort to prove you were right.

However, this time, you took a breath. You realized their cruelty was about their pain, not your worth. You stayed silent. You protected your peace.

- The feeling: It doesn't feel like a rush of adrenaline. It feels like a quiet, solid ground beneath your feet.

2. The Trophy of Resilience

You win this on Tuesday morning when you are heartbroken, grieving, or overwhelmed. You don't want to get out of bed. The blanket feels like the only safe place in the world.

Then you throw the covers off. You put your feet on the floor, make the coffee, and answer the email. You show up. Nobody clapped. Nobody handed you a medal for "Getting Out of Bed," but it was a heroic act. You saved yourself that day.

3. The Trophy of Disappointing Others

This is the hardest trophy to earn, especially for women. You win this when you finally say "No."

You say no to the committee. You say no to the event you hate. You say no to the family obligation that drains you. You choose to disappoint someone else rather than betraying yourself.

- The feeling: At first, it feels like guilt, but if you sit with it, the guilt transforms into self-respect.

The Withdrawal from Applause

We have to be honest about one thing: Earning invisible trophies can feel lonely.

Our egos are addicted to applause. We are conditioned to believe that if nobody saw it, it didn't happen. When you do the hard work of character building, when you forgive someone who isn't sorry, or when you work hard on a project that gets no recognition; part of you wants to scream.

Part of you wants to say, *"Does anyone see how mature I am being right now? Does anyone see how hard I am trying?"*

This is the withdrawal symptom of the ego. It is painful. It feels like you are vanishing but this is the crucible.

This is the moment you switch fuel sources. You stop running on the cheap, sugary fuel of other people's opinions, and you start running on the clean, nuclear energy of self-respect.

Foundation vs. Decoration

Think of your life as a house.

Visible trophies are the decorations. They are the chandelier, the expensive curtains, and the fresh paint. They look beautiful to the neighbors.

Invisible trophies are the foundation. They are the steel beams inside the walls. They are the plumbing. They are the insulation.

You can have a house with a stunning chandelier, but if the foundation is cracked (if you have no integrity, no resilience, no peace), the house will eventually collapse. On the other hand, if you have a strong foundation, you can survive the storm. You can sit in the dark, without the chandelier, and still be safe.

The Ripple Effect

Here is the secret that makes the invisibility bearable: Invisible trophies create a visible atmosphere.

People might not see your trophies, but they feel your presence.

- Because you earned the Trophy of Healing, your children grow up in a house without walking on eggshells. They don't know you did the work to break the cycle, but they feel the safety.

- Because you earned the Trophy of Restraint, your workplace is less toxic. Your colleagues don't know you swallowed your anger, but they feel the calm.

Your internal victories become the external safety for everyone around you. You become the thermostat of the room, setting the temperature to "peace."

Your Private Trophy Room

I want you to imagine a room in your heart.

Take down the plaques that say, "Best Employee" or "Perfect Mother" or "Most Popular." They are gathering dust anyway.

Instead, fill the walls with your private victories. Hang up the moment you forgave the person who never apologized. Hang up the moment you let go of a dream that wasn't yours. Hang up the moment you learned to like the face you see in the mirror.

These trophies don't shine. They don't glitter, yet they are made of something much stronger than gold. They are made of character, and unlike the visible trophies, these are the ones you get to keep forever.

Chapter 20
Time as a Currency

For years, I treated time like an enemy.

I fought against the clock. I raced it. I tried to beat it.

I tried to squeeze thirty hours into a twenty-four-hour day. I lived with a constant, low-grade hum of panic, a feeling that I was behind, that I was forgetting something, that I was failing simply because I was resting.

I was always living five minutes in the future.

If I was washing the dishes, I was mentally writing an email. If I was driving to work, I was mentally holding a meeting. If I was playing with my children, I was mentally checking the clock to see when bedtime was.

I was everywhere except here.

However, there is a shift that happens when you cross the threshold into the second half of life. You stop wanting to beat the clock, and you start wanting to make peace with it.

You realize that rushing is a form of violence against your own soul.

The Addiction to Urgency

We have to ask ourselves: Why do we rush? Even when we aren't late, we rush. We walk fast. We talk fast. We scroll fast.

I realized that I was addicted to urgency because urgency felt like purpose.

If I was rushing, I felt important. If I was stressed, I felt needed. Adrenaline is a powerful drug, and our culture deals it out on every street corner. We are taught that "busy" is a synonym for "worthy."

But when you stop rushing, you have to confront the quiet, and the quiet can be terrifying because it asks the hard questions: *Are you happy? Does this life fit you? Who are you when you aren't fixing everything?*

Rushing is a shield. Slowing down is the act of putting the shield down and letting life actually touch you.

The Myth of "Someday"

We all have a dusty shelf in the back of our minds called "Someday."

- *Someday* I will wear the expensive perfume (I don't want to waste it).
- *Someday* I will take that trip.
- *Someday* I will learn to paint.
- *Someday* I will forgive myself.

We act as if we are going to live forever. We treat our dreams like fine porcelain that is too precious to use, so we keep them locked in a cabinet for a special occasion.

Although the realization of the exhale is this: Today is the special occasion.

The fact that you woke up this morning is a special occasion. The fact that your lungs are filling with air is the event.

I stopped saving the good candles. I burn them on Tuesdays while I'm folding laundry. I stopped saving the "good wine" for guests; I drink it with a pizza on a hard day. I stopped saving my love, my words, and my forgiveness. I use them now. I use them up.

The Garden Gate (A New Way to Say "No")

Think of your time not as money, but as a garden.

In our twenties and thirties, we leave the garden gate wide open. We let anyone walk in. We let strangers trample the flower beds. We say "yes" to every request because we are trying to prove that we are accommodating, energetic, and capable. We are trying to grow a jungle.

Except now? Now, we close the gate.

This isn't because we are mean. It isn't because we are bitter It is because we have finally realized how precious the garden is.

We realize that every time we say "yes" to something that drains us; the committee we hate, the drama we don't need, the obligation that feels like a stone in our shoe, we are letting weeds choke out the roses.

Closing the gate is an act of love for what is growing inside.

When you say, *"No, I can't do that,"* you are not rejecting the other person. You are protecting the quiet space you need to be a kind human being. You are choosing to bloom rather than to wither from exhaustion.

The Art of Lingering

There is a lost art that I am trying to reclaim: Lingering.

To linger is to stay longer than necessary. It is the opposite of efficiency.

- It is sitting at the dinner table for twenty minutes after the plates are empty, just listening to the conversation.
- It is staying in the shower until the water turns cold.
- It is standing in the driveway looking at the moon before you go inside to start the evening chores.

Efficiency is for machines. Lingering is for humans.

When you linger, you signal to your nervous system that you are safe. You signal that the tiger is not chasing you. You signal that life is not a task to be completed, but a meal to be savored.

JOMO (The Joy of Missing Out)

You have heard of FOMO, the Fear Of Missing Out. It is that anxious feeling that everyone else is having more fun than you.

I want to introduce you to JOMO: The Joy Of Missing Out.

It is the exquisite pleasure of knowing there is a party happening somewhere, and you are not at it. You are in your pajamas. You are reading a book. You are drinking tea, and you are exactly where you want to be.

It is the relief of realizing that you don't need to be everywhere to be whole. You don't need to know every piece of news. You don't need to be "relevant."

You just need to be real.

The Hourglass

I don't look at the calendar with fear anymore. I look at it with reverence.

I know the sand is running through the hourglass. I can't stop it. I can't flip it back over, but I can choose how I watch the sand fall.

I can watch it with panic, trying to catch every grain, or I can watch it with gratitude, marveling at how beautiful the grains are as they slip through.

So, to you please …

Eat the cake. Buy the shoes. Say the words "I love you" first.

Hug your friends for three seconds longer than is socially acceptable.

Do not save your life for later.

Live it right now, in the messy, beautiful, fleeting glory of today.

Chapter 21
The Beauty of the Finite
(Making Friends with Mortality)

In the first half of life, we live as if we are immortal.

We treat time as an infinite resource. We treat our bodies as invincible machines. We say, *"I'll do that later,"* assuming there is always a later. We assume the people we love will always be there.

However, in the second half, usually somewhere around the time we lose a parent, or a friend gets a scary diagnosis, or we simply see the texture of our own neck change in the mirror, the math changes.

We realize that the runway is not endless.

Most people react to this with terror. This is the root of the "Midlife Crisis."

We buy the sports car to prove we are fast. We get the surgery to prove we are young. We run faster to outpace the end.

Except, the "Sixth Sky" perspective offers a different approach. Instead of running from the deadline, we turn and face it, and we realize something profound: The deadline is what gives the project value.

The Frame Makes the Picture

I want you to imagine going to an art museum. You walk up to a beautiful painting, but you notice something strange. The canvas doesn't end. It stretches out of the frame, across the wall, out the door, and over the horizon. It goes on forever.

Would that be art, or would it just be wallpaper?

What makes a painting beautiful is the frame. The limit gives it focus. The fact that the artist had to choose exactly what to put inside those four edges is what gives the image meaning.

Death is the frame of life.

The fact that this life will end is exactly what makes it precious.

- The coffee tastes better because you won't drink it forever.
- The hug feels warmer because you know you won't hold this person forever.
- The sunset is stunning specifically because it is disappearing.

If the sunset stayed fixed in the sky for 24 hours a day, we wouldn't even look up. We would close the blinds. We only watch it because it is fleeting.

The Thought Experiment: The Endless Vacation

Imagine you went on a vacation to Gold Coast, and someone told you: *"You can never leave. You have to stay here for a million years."*

At first, you'd be thrilled, but by year 10? By year 100? You would stop looking at the ocean. You would stop savoring the prawns. You would become bored, lethargic, and numb. The urgency of joy would vanish.

Scarcity creates value. Diamonds are valuable because they are rare. Your Mondays are valuable because you only get a finite number of them (about 4,000 in an average life).

When you make friends with your own mortality, you stop wasting time. You don't hold grudges because you realize: *I literally do not have the budget for anger.* You become ruthless about your joy.

Mono no Aware (The Pathos of Things)

The Japanese have a beautiful phrase for this: *Mono no aware*

It translates roughly to "the pathos of things," or a sensitivity to the ephemeral nature of beauty. It is why they celebrate the Cherry Blossom season. The blossoms are not beautiful *despite* the fact that they fall; they are beautiful *because* they fall.

When we look in the mirror at 50, we often see "fading" but *Mono no aware* invites us to see "blooming."

We are in the autumn of our year. The leaves are turning gold and red. They are more vibrant now than they were when they were green. Yes, they will fall, but my god, look at the color.

Emotional Death Cleaning

There is a Swedish practice called *Döstädning*, or "Death Cleaning." It refers to decluttering your house, so your family doesn't have to deal with your junk when you are gone.

So, I want to propose Emotional Death Cleaning.

When you realize your time is finite, you want to travel light.

- You clear out the junk of old resentments.
- You toss out the clutter of "what people think."
- You sweep away the dust of regret.

You want your internal house to be clean. You want to be able to sit in the center of your soul and feel the breeze coming through the open windows, unblocked by piles of emotional hoarding.

Breaking the Good Dishes

So, how does this change our Tuesday afternoon?

It changes the "Someday" shelf. We all have things we are saving for a special occasion. The expensive perfume, the good plates, the heartfelt letter we mean to write.

Mortality whispers in your ear: "Use it now."

- Wear the silk dress to the grocery store.
- Burn the $50 candle while you pay bills.
- Tell your friend you love her today, not at her eulogy.

Living with an awareness of death does not make you morbid. It makes you vibrant. It makes you present. It makes you the most alive person in the room, because you are the only one who realizes that the clock is ticking, and the game is to enjoy every single second on the clock.

Chapter 22
The Second Innocence

(Redefining Hope)

By the time we reach 45, we have seen some things. We have watched marriages implode. We have seen corporations lay off loyal employees. We have seen leaders lie. We have had our hearts broken by people we trusted. We have seen how the sausage is made, and frankly, we have lost our appetite or became vegetarians.

The natural, almost biological reaction to this accumulation of data is Cynicism.

Cynicism feels smart. It feels protective. It wears a leather jacket and smokes a cigarette in the corner, rolling its eyes at the naive people who still believe in fairy tales. The cynic says, *"I won't get my hopes up, so I can't be hurt."* The cynic says, *"I know how this ends, so I won't even start."*

In the first half of life, we often lose our innocence. We get hardened. We build a shell.

However, the work of the "Exhale" is to crack that shell open; not to return to the naivety of childhood, but to advance to something far more powerful: The Second Innocence.

The Three Stages of Trust

To understand where we are going, we have to look at the map of the human heart.

1. The First Innocence (Naivety) This is the child. You trust because you don't know any better. You believe the world is good because you haven't met the bad parts yet. This is beautiful, but it is fragile. One rock can shatter it.

2. Cynicism (The Wound) This is where most adults get stuck. You have been hit by the rock. You survive, but you vow never to be vulnerable again. You mistake your scar tissue for wisdom. You think that being suspicious makes you safe.

Except, here is the truth: Cynicism is lazy. It takes zero effort to roll your eyes at the world. It takes zero courage to expect the worst.

3. The Second Innocence (Wisdom) This is the destination. This is the woman who knows the world is broken, who knows people can be cruel, who knows that loss is inevitable... and still chooses to be delighted by the moon. Still chooses to trust. Still chooses to hope.

This is not blindness. This is defiance.

Optimism vs. Hope

We often confuse Hope with Optimism, but they are very different things.

- Optimism is the belief that things will turn out well. It is often a passive wish. *"Everything happens for a reason!"* Sometimes, this is toxic, because sometimes things *don't* turn out well.
- Hope is not a prediction of the future; it is a declaration of allegiance in the present.

Vaclav Havel, the writer and statesman, said: *"Hope is definitely not the same thing as optimism. It is not the conviction that something will turn out well, but the certainty that something makes sense, regardless of how it turns out."*

The Second Innocence relies on Hope. It says, *"I am going to plant this garden, not because I am guaranteed a harvest, but because the act of planting is good for my soul."*

The Rebellion of Awe

When you have been cynical for a long time, the Second Innocence feels like a rebellion.

It is a rebellion against the grey, numbing fog of adulthood. It requires you to reclaim your Awe.

Remember when you were five, and a dandelion was the most amazing thing you had ever seen? You blew on it and watched the seeds fly, and it was magic. Then you turned thirty, and a dandelion became a weed. It became a nuisance to be poisoned.

The Second Innocence is kneeling down on the grass at age fifty, picking the dandelion, and blowing on it again. It is letting yourself be stunned by the fact that seeds fly.

It is looking at your partner of twenty years, the one who chews too loudly and forgets to take out the trash, and suddenly seeing them as a miraculous, breathing human being who chose to walk through life with you.

Softening the Fist

Cynicism makes your hands curl into fists. You are ready to fight. You are ready to defend. The Second Innocence opens the hand.

Try this physical practice. When you feel yourself getting bitter, when you are watching the news, or listening to a difficult relative, check your hands. Are they tight?

Consciously open them. Palms up. This signals to your brain: *"I am not afraid. I am open to surprise. I am open to grace."*

The Risk of Being a Fool

The biggest fear we have about dropping our cynicism is that we will look like fools.

- *"If I get excited and it fails, I'll look stupid."*
- *"If I trust him and he betrays me, I'll look weak."*

The Second Innocence says: Let them call me a fool.

I would rather be the fool who loved too much than the genius who loved too little. I would rather be the fool who got excited about a sunset than the cool person who didn't look up from their phone. I would rather have a broken heart than a heart that never beat at all.

The Return of Color

When you live in Cynicism, the world is black and white. It is safe, but it is boring. When you step into the Second Innocence, the color returns.

It is Technicolor. It is vibrant. Yes, the pain hurts more, but the joy feels deeper. The coffee tastes better. The music sounds richer.

You have walked through the fire of the first half of life. You didn't burn up. You just burned off the things that didn't matter. Now, you are standing in the ash, holding a flower. You know the fire is real, but you also know the flower is real.

And you choose the flower.

Chapter 23
The Legacy of Ripples
(Redefining Impact)

We are obsessed with the word "Legacy."

We want to leave a mark. We want to put our name on a building.

We want to write a bestseller. We want to be remembered.

Deep down, this desire comes from a fear of erasure. We worry that if we don't build a monument to our existence it will be as if we were never here at all. We want to carve our initials into the tree of history.

However the "Sixth Sky" perspective teaches us something humbling:

Monuments crumble. Ripples travel.

If you build a stone statue of yourself, eventually the rain will wear down the face. Eventually, the name at the base will be unreadable. The "Great Men" of history are often forgotten, or worse, their statues become hollow homes for pigeons.

But energy? Energy never dies. It just transfers.

The Physics of Kindness

I want you to imagine a still pond. You pick up a small stone and throw it into the center. *Plunk.* The stone sinks. It disappears. It hits the bottom and settles into the mud.

However, on the surface, something is happening. A ring of water expands, then another, then another. The ripples move outward, touching the reeds on the shore, disturbing a dragonfly, rocking a lily pad.

You are the stone.

You might feel small. You might feel like you are sinking into the mud of obscurity. You might feel like your life is quiet, but you have no idea how far your ripples are traveling.

The Chaos Theory of Goodness

There is a concept in science called the "Butterfly Effect", the idea that a butterfly flapping its wings in India can cause a storm in Southeast Asia. Small causes have massive effects.

I believe in the Chaos Theory of Goodness.

- You smiled at a stressed cashier in the grocery store. You didn't yell when she made a mistake.
- Just because you were patient, her cortisol levels dropped. She went home feeling human instead of hunted.

- Just because she felt human, she had the energy to read a book to her son instead of putting him in front of the TV.
- Just because she read to him, he went to school the next day feeling loved and secure.
- Just because he felt secure, he defended a kid who was being bullied on the playground.

You will never know that little boy's name. You will never know you saved him from a bad day. You are the stone at the bottom of the pond, but you changed the future.

The Invisible Inheritance

We worry about what we are leaving our children or the next generation in terms of money or property, but the most important inheritance is Emotional Inheritance.

- If you do the work to heal your trauma, you stop the cycle of abuse. That is a legacy.
- If you learn to regulate your nervous system, you create a home that feels safe. That safety enters the bones of your children (or your nieces, or your students). They grow up with a baseline of calm. That is a legacy.
- If you are the woman who laughs loudly and eats the cake, you give permission to every younger woman watching you to enjoy her life. That is a legacy.

We leave behind an atmosphere.

Making Peace with Anonymity

The ego hates this chapter. The ego wants credit. The ego wants the plaque on the wall.

The Softening requires us to make peace with **Anonymity.**

Think about the people who have shaped you. The teacher who told you were smart in 3rd grade. The stranger who helped you change a tire in the rain. The grandmother who hummed while she cooked.

Do you know their resumes? Do you know their net worth? No. You remember how they made you feel.

Maya Angelou said it best: *"People will forget what you said, people will forget what you did, but people will never forget how you made them feel."*

To be anonymous is not to be unimportant. The sun is anonymous, it doesn't sign its name in the sky every morning, but without it, we would all die.

Being Contagious

So, instead of trying to be "Famous," let's try to be **Contagious.**

We are biologically wired to mimic each other. If you walk into a room with tense shoulders and a scowl, everyone tightens up, but if you walk into a room with a soft belly and an open face, you act as a tuning fork. You set the tone.

- Be contagious with calm.
- Be contagious with grace.

- Be contagious with the refusal to rush.

In a world that is sick with anxiety, your peace is a medicine. You don't need to force-feed it to anyone; you just need to embody it.

The Final Ripple

One day, you will be gone. The stone will be at the bottom of the pond, but the water will still be moving.

The love you gave will be circulating in the hearts of people you knew, and they will pass it on to people they know, who will pass it on to people who aren't even born yet.

You don't need to carve your name in stone. You just need to throw yourself into the water. Don't hold back. Love is the only thing that multiplies when you give it away.

Chapter 24
The Sixth Sky

We have traveled a long way together on these pages.

We started in the basement, weighed down by heavy suitcases of resentment and the exhausting armor of the "Nice Girl." We walked through the dark, confusing Hallway of Realignment. We sat by the Campfire, warming our hands with a new kind of ambition. We looked our mortality in the eye and decided to buy the flowers anyway.

Now, where does all this work leave us?

If we are no longer fighting, and we are no longer rushing, and we are no longer performing... where are we?

We have arrived at the **Sixth Sky**.

The Geography of Your Soul

I want you to visualize your life not as a timeline, but as an altitude.

The First Sky is the ground floor. This is where most of the world lives. It is the realm of reaction. In the First

Sky, the fog is thick. You can't see two feet in front of you. Every obstacle looks like a mountain.

- This is where the traffic jam ruins your day.
- This is where a rude comment from a stranger feels like a knife in your chest.
- This is where you are constantly fighting to prove you are right, pulling on the rope until your hands bleed.

It is loud down there. It is humid with drama. It is exhausting.

However, the work you have done; the shedding, the softening, the "No," acts as an elevator. It lifts you up.

The Sixth Sky is the altitude of **Wisdom**.

It is not a place you go when you die. It is a place you can inhabit while you are still very much alive, doing your laundry and paying your bills.

It is the place where the air is clear.

The View From the Window

Have you ever looked out the window of an airplane as it breaks through the cloud cover?

Down below, it is raining, it is grey, it is stormy but up here, the sun has been shining the whole time. The sun never stopped shining; you just couldn't see it from the ground.

From the Sixth Sky, your problems haven't disappeared, the traffic is still there, the difficult relative is still there, the bills are still there, but your relationship to them has changed.

You are no longer in the traffic; you are watching it. You see the red taillights. You see the chaos but you feel a strange, detached compassion. You realize: *"Ah, look at all those people rushing. Look at all that fear. I remember what that felt like."*

The things that used to destroy you: rejection, wrinkles, and mistakes now look like tiny toys on a game board. They have lost their power to knock you over.

You Are the Sky, Not the Weather

This is the most vital realization of the Sixth Sky, and if you take only one thing from this book, let it be this:

You are the sky. You are not the weather.

In the first half of life, we identify with the weather. A storm of sadness comes, and we say, *"I am depressed."* A tornado of anger comes, and we say, *"I am furious."* We let the weather consume us. We think we are the clouds.

However, in the Sixth Sky, you realize you are the vast, blue expanse behind the clouds.

Clouds come. They are inevitable. Grief will come. Fear will come. The storms will rage, and they will be loud and wet and scary, but the sky does not break. The sky makes space for the storm, allows it to pass, and remains unchanged.

When you live from this place, you become untouchable. Someone can project their anger onto you (a storm cloud), and you can say, *"I see a storm passing through."* You don't have to grab the thunder and stuff it in your pocket. You can just let it float by.

Dual Citizenship

Now, here is the challenge. We cannot float in the clouds forever. We have bodies. We have mortgages. We have to go down to the First Sky to handle the logistics of being human.

The goal is Dual Citizenship.

You live in the First Sky, but you keep your passport from the Sixth Sky in your back pocket.

- You are washing the dishes (First Sky activity), but your mind is swimming in gratitude (Sixth Sky mindset).
- You are dealing with a crisis at work (First Sky setting), but you have "dropped the rope" and refuse to panic (Sixth Sky perspective).

When the world tries to pull you back into the mud, when the "Nice Girl" tries to resurrect herself, or the "General Manager" tries to take control, you have a tool.

The Elevator Button.

In a moment of stress, close your eyes. Visualize pressing the button for the 6th floor. Ask yourself: *"Does this matter at 30,000 feet?"*

Does the snarky email matter at 30,000 feet? *No.* Does the burnt dinner matter? *No.* Does the love I have for my child matter? *Yes.*

The elevator takes you up. The noise fades. The priorities realign.

The Lighthouse Effect

When you start living from this altitude, you change the atmosphere around you.

Remember the **Ripple Effect**? This is where it begins.

People are drawn to those who have visited the Sixth Sky. In a world that is screaming, your silence becomes a shelter. In a world that is rushing, your slowness becomes a permission slip.

You become a Lighthouse. A lighthouse doesn't run around the island looking for boats to save. It doesn't scream at the storm. It just stands there. It shines. It stays put.

And by simply being who you are, unhurried, unbothered, and kind, you show others where the rocks are. You show them the way home.

The Final Exhale

My friend,

You have outgrown the woman you used to be.

Do not try to squeeze back into her skin. It doesn't fit anymore.

You have permission to be this new version of yourself.

You have permission to be softer, slower, and wiser.

You have permission to disappoint the people who only wanted you for your utility.

You have permission to enjoy your life, right now, before the painting is finished.

The heavy suitcase is on the ground. The garden gate is closed. The fire is lit.

Take a breath.

Look up.

The view is beautiful from here.

Welcome to the Exhale.